# A Nest This Size

# Aidan Fine

# A Nest This Size

Shearsman Books

*Second Edition.*
Published in the United Kingdom in 2020 by
Shearsman Books Ltd
PO Box 4239
Swindon
SN3 9FN

Shearsman Books Ltd Registered Office
30–31 St. James Place, Mangotsfield, Bristol BS16 9JB
*(this address not for correspondence)*

www.shearsman.com

ISBN 978-1-84861-736-0

Cover image: 'A Sociable Weaver's nest in Namibia', by Jacynth Roode.
Copyright © Jacynth Roode, 2009.

ACKNOWLEDGMENTS
Credit to the editor of the online journal *Moria* in which the poem "Dear
Rabbit" first appeared, and to Action, Yes! Press for the publication of 'On
the firmament of many names', 'Diary Operating Manual(ly) One, Two
and Three', and 'Architectis Moderatis'.

I am unreasonably blessed and deeply grateful for the love and friendship
that keeps me alive and writing, so Thank you Mom, my sister Tree and
son Zay, Kate, Trish, Liz, CJ & Jeff, Christi Brooke Martin, Liza and Jeff,
Annie & Tomasso, Leighann Vanauker, Morgan Schuldt, Kate Street
and (not least) Rhonda & Terri.

# Contents

*for Lise Goett*

"Mockingbirds don't do one thing but make music for us to enjoy. They don't eat up people's gardens, don't nest in corncribs, they don't do one thing but sing their hearts out for us. That's why it's a sin to kill a mockingbird."

Harper Lee

# Pillow Inquiry

"One small room, wooden floor, favorite window.
The leaves are burning. Why should it be better."
—*Kate Greenstreet*

Which pillow did you want on the boat with you
on the way to your sacred conundrums?

You mean to heel, don't you?

Maybe you'll choose the piece stitched in
parabola's fabulous theme-park handiwork?
The one taken down from the avalanche of advertisements?

Which pillow doesn't matter, at this point.

Not when our wanderlust's satchel has grown heavy at our backs
full with the day's actual ridiculum;

                    arguments as pillows impossible to have,
unlikely bearing any weight—

Either way—such tedium—I have swallowed it like pillows.
A pillow full of guilt, a pillow full of medicine of sleep,

                                                    or smother?

Isn't there a no-man's land where
United Nations soldiers, rolling around in jeeps
over marked roads, talk on radios
someone neutral listens to?

I can't believe in them. Military pillows.
Political pillows. How puffy are these pillows?

Pillows in a hovel, pillows hunkered down on dope.
Pillows put in a pretty coffin for the beloved.

I suppose there are some rewards to killing,
but can't see how they trickle down to the living.

No-one's keeping watch this far away, this far off
the grid of daily primetime chum
sucked down without chewing [practically]
by American hearth sharks
who may as well wear barbed wire wrist watches and speedbags
for belt buckles
as they praise the God of Friday in the church of fried chicken
and ball game.
O, pillow talk.

Why so harsh or tidy?

Isn't there a small house in Maine where my friend
Monika grows tomatoes
and writes poems to her boyfriend's penis
in noodles on the wall?

I got a letter once that almost said that
and it was from Monika it said in the softest ink.

Or maybe it was goose eggs in a frying pan (cast iron of course)
as he lay on her pillows in her bed, in her living-room-
bed, and a season of snow thought all about the house
until the house was thoughtfully pillowed in.

In the human body there are so many pillows
and yet none enough to break one's fall
from a building, or a boyfriend, or a knife.
Is the bone a kind of pillow?

Is a tooth a pillow? If it was what a treat
for the tooth fairy to find in sleep
for sleep to rest the jaw and relax
your maw upon the down

                                    within.


A little money under the pillow, for the trouble
                    of pulling it out.


[Note: We are writing in for a full refund—when we write.]
Come then; the grave is a pillow.

The brick that fell and landed on the bed.
A pill is a pillow and a pond for swans
is a pillow, and the dew is
a pillow for the morning light.

Finger pads are pillows for feeling
and remarkable in singularity
for every time they touch they leave a note
in circular language—*Nautilusian.*

I had a lover once, whose eyes
were pillows and lids were rumpled
sheets, and she smelled like unwashed hair.
The footnote is a pillow, for the over thought.

The belly of man is a pillow, right? At least, mine is.

A character in a book is a pillow, especially rabbit,
in children's books, who is always hopping. The rail is a pillow
for the train's smooth thundering path and plane;

the clouds above—of course.

Kind of them, to pillow the sky forth
through all these sleepy days.

\*

To lift the head from the pillow—to wonder—have we been
too long the same?

# Dear Diary Manual

Xxxx Xxxxx,

I miss you.

The dust doesn't care but to cover flat surfaces meticulously.
None the less; I forget what for. Is it missing I am doing? These
fingertips cake after a brief pressing down until they are with.
An after matter to be rubbed away. Impractical and rude. So a
sleuth of wind (a secret measurement self sacredized) interjects
meaning to a room. A room I live in with or without you: how
small matters.

Never mind. I will replace you permanently with another diary.
I will replace you with one which has no operating manual.
It would be much too arduous, in fact impossible to write [a
manual]. I make no excuse, and this is just that. Such a thing
makes me feel so *therefore*-ish, congenially speaking. In other
words one considers the tasks at hand. To be proper, I will
operate the manual while I replace you. For synchronicity
practice. This will go on for as long as it has to in order to
dissolve my abandonment issuing. I am in one valid mood
about you continuously. I like to say definitely, but if I speak ill
I trust you will keep a record.

This is less a superficial homage than you might leap to argue.
Please listen, to these illicit figures I pronounce by construct; I
mean I construct them this way (figuratively), for a very dark
reason that counts. I have imagined you over, many a time.
And I am no Aristotle. (Nor Pope, nor Valéry, nor Homer).

I imagine this whole thing is an *idea*: your manual of operation. A manual in which I will attempt to express a nature separate from which you represent—specifically for the purpose of protecting my sensitive areas [in particular whatever immortal parts of me remain undead]—from which (yes, again) you represent. As a Diary of course: nothing less. You must remain utterly hypothetical, and I must love you or I don't. You are conditional and you have been verified. There is mercury in the barometer you are, holding as still as a bullet. But holding still, as a bullet cannot. Do you recognize the slight grammatical difference between *bullet* and *mercury*…(holy perpetual motion!)

One question haunts me; will you still allow me to humor you? I am trying so hard to remember my station: You used to laugh. I remember your racecar-fast eyes forgetting to come to a conclusion—those were happier times. But then, the rules were general, the contradictions mildly pathetic, and the galaxies continuously flashing above weighed *immensity, eternity, infinity*. All these wor(l)ds were inescapable. I wonder if I should use them in the manual. I wasn't thinking of that. But I will consider this, and also types of automobiles.

I do not know if there will be a moral to your story. This will eventually be converted into a limitation, and thereby particularized in random creation. Tit for tat. I will distribute the episodes, each as an assertion—not a proposition—which will become square in time.

Yesterday was a good day is not as true as it was Tuesday. I am bound to be consistently inferring this way to maintain a balance. Mine, dear Diary. So please commence imagining a faith for us. One that frees God from page numbers. I will count on the sound it makes to guide me, but then . . . other sounds too.

# On the firmament of many names

d d,

In my sleep I was told by a sleeper cell you must not be called Diary anymore. Now, whether it came from an ethereal daybed or an insidious apse in my lexicon, doesn't matter. The cell slept, and the cell didn't show: its message sounded snore. Instead, crosswords appeared—larynx across, and yes—down. Daisies were daubed in the miniature airspace above that, and there was a peal of bells. Later, nothing moved again. Eventually, in a springing breadth of light, appeared—ligature across, and game down.

And so I woke obedience. Also, I woke obedience and astronomy; I woke obedience and astronomy and music. I said look. I said I think Diary is a meteorite and a diploma and future . . . responsibility falls on all of us . . . so everyone please turn around. So we didn't face each other during the imagining exercise a long time. Grief made us want to, at moments, but we fought like hell, stoics against hell. *Grief because there are too many names. Grief because each one is good and then vanishes.* The lists thronged. The lists carried torches of fire . . . I woke myself.

When I opened my eyes I knew this would be a ferial day. I would make certain not to gaze at screens or other vehicles of bafflement. I would put on clothes. I would put clothes away. I would put water on the dirt my plants lived in, and try not to feel so venerable. Images of your face upbraided newly thin air. Standing still amidst owned objects, to me I acted like a solar system: a bigot of space. Your face became faces. I said I am a bigot, I bigot, I am big. Bigger than you Diary. I absorbed sentimental humidity as an absence. An uncommon thirst doubled over. I resisted missing you again but was not certain what that meant. In this way I failed at longing. So the burden of your replacement pressed again.

Then an urgency to write for words. Send off for a stratagem to gain spectral crystallization.

Questions renew: *Are you forensic anymore? Are you a solution of loose nucleotides? Are you going to photograph well in this light? Does your geometry spell a prayer only children's inner ears understand?*

Theory and tests, theory and tests: these are the nearest neighborhood frequencies I associated with the great number of names. If I am the messenger how could you listen? How can you hear me when I do not know what you will be called? I am contained by too many answers.

I leave the house quickly. I leave with the assembly:

*Rabbit; zigzag; glove; bishop; seashell; wave from nowhere; horseback…*

# Diary operating manual(ly)

[Data entry—9/2006]

1. Death or Ceremony of carriage; methods of getting at remembrances:

At the moment blank is added, the end will be expected to contain emptiness in various states of completion. Some time later some (to be left to measure) many blanks should be finished emptying, and will each of these cast off into the void. If the blanks are assembled in ordinary sequences, they should be labeled at their breaking points. And meaningful ones will be (difficult). Thus the blanks which are most nearly complete at the moment when nothing is added should receive the least label, and those only beginning to grow will receive the most. Among any triptych set of blanks, which will now be isolated from an assembled mourning set, cast off by less affable blanks; the blanks situated near the beginning point of the assembly should be in agreement with any expectation. Ignore the rate of reaction which is all extra, but measure all corresponding rememberments. Lastly replace blanks with souls. Realizing should, upon assertion, possible.

2. Remember the pages were consisting of arms, legs, foreheads, anterior torsos and thumbs when amassing emotion. Lie broken spine down as lovingly. Lay rheumatic hands on the cover to coax experience carefully (one understands the other).

3. Leftover quills go in the mouth.

4. What is dead is neither belonging to what was, nor indicating in any way, a past inhabitation or summary of any mineral composition. Not merely and/or not, or mostly not, a target.

5. Regard a defect in every mourners' eye. Regard style of art. Regard subject and subject's strength. *What is a thunderfish? What is that sound of thunder?*

6. New testaments present moments featuring everyone.

7. Somewhere [in here] is a vast improvement.

## Architectis Moderatis

Now I'd like to make a slew of curious statements pretty quickly, until the keys come. I beg you to bear with my assembling helices, [incensed and heated to keep you) and/or bring your density and gradients along with their eyes: please. O, plenty of materials, of course. Hammers and nails and I will be delivered sometime soon, but you don't think we should wait any longer—not really.

I still don't know your name, or I you, though I do consider a sacred annealment tangible. A kind of recovery we might rasp at strangers' doors after a long afternoon parade. In the little city I strode alongside a similar haunting, sober, as if to pose a better spy. The eyes seemed exhausted, but spoke of you fondly. Tilting a head toward the refuge of shadow, I took it all in. "O," I thought, "you won't scare anyone that way." In awhile and along the way we eventually come to wonder how we know each other so oddly well, aloud.

How were you everywhere that day, like a lack of air, and somehow, never needless? The walls of the little city grown largely over the rivers. I felt like an open angle then, and my arches carefully intermitted. The problems laid mad doggedly down, then an aqueduct-like system or cumbersome relic of longing. I did feel some friction against my heritage . . . I wanted a drink.

But, since your's is a thirst only this denatured drink offers itself to, then, I will inhabit this radio of clime, and will be mindful of the static gaps in any terrific weather. It will be alright right? Please get up and do not beware of too much.

The fragmenting of this theme [Dear Diary] into its own
motives may soon suffer momentum's pitch, but you will help
me commend creation for knowing its architecture I trust? Help
me praise the moonbeam for putting up angles of calculated
surprise, and importing us through edificial quantities of sleep.
Praise the forbidden machine of memory for crashing . . .

Every testimony of the fog is both regional and virtual. So
you are not a love letter; you are a blustering idea of wind.
Apocryphal, unreliable, puerile, and fantastic. I grow to love
the elemental functionality of our zigzagging model. I grow
stagnant. Together we've become subject to the storm of X-ray,
still so here; I volunteer our broken whims this glass solution.

Thankfully, we were born without mechanical regulation of
our [glottal and ungulate] trifle registers: This may soon mean
deconstruction is likely over time, so here comes *why do we
crave our undoing?* [and] *Who taught us to desire?* Framed by the
window of any houses here; we are free, and the dull repetition
of our infamy is a famous, but finished, problem. Look how
stupid this city is. It actually attempts to celebrate itself! They
say; *traffic is a joke.* I say real (is) funny.

When stalled at the light, when the woodlands up my sleeves
shiver; they want to give me away. I press their fury green tips
inward, I am awkward. They stab. I am impressed to bevel
away at my nature. It's the way in or out, I'm not sure. It is
hard work, and no I am not a cheerful edge. I am tendered
by moveable commerce: life doesn't owe life lost. But if flown
outward too far, like hell, it will.

At any moment, under whatever oblique frontispiece hung here,
we may hang wildly over into primal dance. Exuberance too,
can make sense of our lost legend. And that's just it: Did you
know the spotted fly-catcher has this many names? Post-bird,

Egypt bird, old man, beam bird, cobweb or bee bird? You know what that means; He *is* a good catch!

But I should not embellish what I am not as if I could. I also know how charming little tunes may habituate the divine. So I send for you each melody I mark. Call you with a star drunk yodel;

Can you come out here in a year?

Time for a ticket.

Don't forget?

And dear, mine; In response to your metonymic letters, my voice is a challenging [antique]; an item that may auctioneer for less than a buck in these parts. It gathers itself by way of introduction, and bouquets like a fist.          Stops here.

Segments of my motives lead to new impetuous dissentions, and segments fantasize: *the pink bowls in your body full of patriotic milk; the life of your hot tongue leaning tired against its teeth*. These mimetic devotions sustain me. Time is on my mime.

Yes, you see. That's how I am believably ignored. The more timid locations in the imagination struggle to harmonize two things (sweet and graceful). Higher Organisms? Say *hello*. Sum of button and which to push:

Precisely midway between the heart and head: a category is born. Brand new. I am told things afterward, that don't help much, so I will not repeat them. Not here but for the synthesis of vital inspirations; which (without labor) ensures that a number (two) of us may be afforded a correct placing on the messenger template:

Category (answer) or no (receipt).

The allegory for *which* has not been written?

I wander still.

# Diary operating manual(ly)

Data entry *[January 2007]*

1.  Send in the bones book rate. Send sport[  ]ships and score
    the slanting. Shipments of making rules.

2.  Automobiles: *immensity, eternity, infinity* [must get to]
    laughter: (an unattractive semblance of letters?) One enjoys
    the dropping of a jaw, and one believes in the vehicle.

3.  Arrivals, conditions, disciplines: What ports of authority
    [Set by? Who says?] have supposed aftermaths? In the
    case of suits, tie them off. Carbon is simple being— also
    faceted, also loveless— Trust its light.

4.  If you believe in God, that he or she may detest even
    numbers may have occurred to you.

5.  Names can demote the cataclysmal properties of their
    own; so fete them in pastoral sceneries to ensure safety of
    nominal conditions—these and wild flowers.

6.  Dearly (Re)beloved: cause to consider the (re) amplifies
    in all sacred scenarios of naming; so ≠ so. Remuneration
    namely repels enumeration. Dear (who), dearly named (to
    be inserted as inspiration) continues from one end of the
    spectrum to the other; as a rule.

7.  To sketch a view along an arbitrary line a deliberate impression is the strongest impression: absolutely not. Negative impressions are made so positive images may eventually be taken by the hand.

8.  Note sketch patterns may divide (attention of) The Following.

9.  Put what in ink! Denote further later.

## ~~Edificial Evidence~~

Do you remember Jacob of Liège of the fourteenth century?

Neither do I.

They say in his time he worried music had become "lascivious
beyond measure." What measure is measure beyond measure?
I have wondered if anyone has a theory besides the church; I
wonder if astronomers have attended any sum sermons. And
if I could get the astronomers to talk to the economists; And if
I could have a slew of indigo children mediate them by game?
Do you think they would come up with a less suitable Theory
of La-scivious-ness?

Beyond measure is my best guess.

When I think of his Liege I see sheets of arabesque catching
fire in a pauper's house. In a field the like one eyeballs from
an airplane. I think of our old school; the dirt floors. I think
of that infinitely recapitulating school-window view. Yes I am
referring to the remote past. Modes, good mode, thank you
(same as now.) This vision injects me with a subtle warfare and
helps maintain my amenable mood of well-being.

Though in your vast absence—and after the skepticisms your
frayed edges caused in the hall—I am affected by a measure of
physical achievement, of simile, of theatre makeup, and some
method I am creating under wraps. My random tantrums have
actually become tonic.

Will I soon seem more capable of determining your uniqueness among the fray? All pressure points to this way to the village yes. Otherwise I am bound to this nightmare and caught in a constant attempt to resemble your murder.

Mind; I am watching after you, and you mustn't but you will fret, though I dwell here with and willing.

My post is set on the point you have marked with your absent fraction. Have you born witness to the scale of these walls? My fever is pitched so high there, reflection proves a mandatory exercise. Fortunately, the walls are fairly built, and they measure themselves: note by note. I sway to God for my mother. Come, come.

Lately.

Without you I will feel crass and obvious. Too obvious. I would rather surmise a doctrine of affections, and mirror what is vivid. Much rather. Sincerely, struggling.

Nothing to panic about, I just know.

p.s. I have enclosed a reasonable religion I have no room for in my workspace. Hide it for me? I trust you will tell no-one you know.

Dear
here,


Is art working too hard where you are? Send him home, and
with his rubble of luggage. (Insert photograph of here).

It is written on these walls that in art worked too hard we
inhabit hell. In diligence we might avoid ourselves and miss
hell. Hell lives in lazy art to which it is impossible to fasten
your attention. Please please, everything says. But how can we
avoid virtuosity and embrace that purposeless brilliance? The
frame hurts the edge of the picture unless it would be too big.
*A visual refrain.* Regardless of more general things like genetics
(which are all tableware and stereo); our temple building affair
would be more than a vogue movement after all. Less than: a
primitive horn made of the noise itself. Speaking of: of.

I won't forget our neighbors who make hay. Our memories
are stacked expertly in the fields of my heart. I wanted to tell
them how battled antiques dream in (in)visible droves. For sale
caricatures of rust and want; I miss them too often, you know.
And miss the monies rumored to cover their cost. When you
come back I hope you'll pick a few of them up on your way.

You wrote: *Announce your lyric little Put; step to the front-of-the-
beat.* And: *Which*

*aspect of music composes in you vertically?* I say timber, quietly,
into my sleeve. I wish you could hear how the music falls.

Sway; you sway. The mountain speaks in your favor. Up and up in a way I am confident in a new category of music, and promise to "come come."

But not now. I'm too busy fighting *the idea of saltpeter*.

Have you heard the song of the seasonal berry? They get good acoustics at the local grocers. I firmly will not let the tune of that song out of my head!

Forgive me. Gossip is a terminal addiction in the area. Honestly, I do accept the fact that the whole thing is entirely unpredictable. Although, I realize the mechanism of art synthesis has here [as elsewhere] been stupefied by my outline of it. I suspect that not too much more inspection is needed for elucidation.

The structural details are written in common code enough, and I come to believe they are "th" sound.

# Diary operating manual(ly)

"This mixture of apparently disparate materials—scandal and spiritualism, current events and eternal recurrences—is not promising on the face of it." —Gary Wills

Data entry 9/2006:

*Retrace.* Or retrograde? Doesn't matter.

A) You were getting climactic in your years, and B) no-one can tell.

1. Again, to stipulate how the myths were punctuated: open wider, take risks, be wise; generally aware of the triumph of lies. It is a tedious theory we practice. This may not be as true as the way we practice tedium, theoretically.

2. The letters came after the war we thought was the one for us. Our memory of it was so familialy confabulated, we had to buy the serial stories of guns so we could stick to them, and count on strangers as if they were kin: justice cuts in line. Follow the woodwind section to opine. For a moment, as brief as any's awe, we assume a lesson is learned for us we will not have to learn en masse, and so we escape narrowly, the consequences of borrowed individuality. Hence, the Dear Diary/episodic corroborations/ occur naturally in situ. The future is all epilogues, starting now.

3. Histrionic is history: repeat and change.

4. Never again look the pages in the eye and say, "you are better without God."

# Very Small Semi-Secret Diary, to Sort of Hide

"I have always thought that a wild animal never looks so well as when some obstacle of pronounced durability is between us. A personal experience has intensified rather than diminished that idea." —Bram Stoker, *Dracula*

Dear Diary: (as) Small

Shhhhh. Do you hear that? I have begun to write by the light of **the**. By now I desperately want to know the answers to every question about the song dynasty I can muster. Like, for instance: Where is the hand strong enough to open the lid, the same which held a simpering figurine of fortune as if alive: Does it hide where missionaries, fit like cowlings to winged fleets, hauled to a sun punished yard, have since become abandoned lovers of mystic friction rusted closed?

I had just the tiniest discussion with a local tree regarding a talent for free associating with our greater aptitude to manhandle foreign miscreants the other day. Minutes went by like nothing at all. Then, with flexible class, said it: repeat, *something beautiful is on the way.*

Draped in a painstaking mask, the sun went on safari then. I wanted to guard what was left of the goldrope with my life: you know the one. No? There is no need to censure beauty in the form of meek crowds prone to silence; Why not bright light? Why not do it pinned-hole camera style in a kitchen in a field and story in some pleasant ships to tilt the view; make a silly homage to discretion: tell them how to float in developer, rooms of things that have a hull, and *keel.* Say: things meant to be friendly but if mistaken for signs of the enemy, will swiftly sink.

A proper disappearance should leave nothing to be desired; get out clean.

Well then? Right brain accept! If all is nothing then a new
challenge has been invited in the form of voided receipts.
I accept assistance from such unfeeled layers via happy
guesswork; but I am careful knowing argument delivered by
pathos will stump our grief. Distinguished grades are blood-
lined on a curve, and subtle changes slum sweetly to invent an
impulse to express.

If to lift your countenance from the fruit bowl nicely, if to kiss
the dusking of frame's emerald surfaces; she may make herself
into a skin of table, of pink-hued patio, of terrible heaps of
sharp edged glass.

She unfills the dark realms rot with crude desire from the
catacombs of her own muscle. The common good's are vowed
to hope of chairs though reach is broken and frails to warn
each rawboned-hand's attempt. This bright surgery must be
conducted with honest word for blade if to successfully present
this to a coughing liniment of tiny throats; I must fall in favor,
if frightened of reminders as familiar as: and almost *kind*—

Slow butterflies ghost through & so arrived, have prematurely
meant what you can never say. A tick: to trick tenderness from
your own tongue. To sleep like a battled babe from whose
dollish mouthing nothing comes. I know well if I don't return
soon we will embed a name in paper napkin rings and set them
over-properly at tables turned toward the guests of ancient
plays performed by little moths that float and glow like fleeting
lessons; lessons you understood once;

*ahhh* but you were a jetty then, a prince, a retro knave affright
of spice and frogs; who dreamt alphabets from pine-bark in the
neighborhood (so trained), and high

on kitchen knives you knew by heart (not an existential art) . . .
and often asked the hand:


*Skin skin, how do I live in your dirty town alive?*

## Optimal normal level of mean impedimenta: original load

"The Machinery, madam, is a term invented by the critics, to signify that part which the deities, angels, or demons, are made to act in the poem." —Alexander Pope

News construed as sing: later, letter, other. (Did the window close? How long was it open?)

A) Take this very word to the mountain and sacrifice it: *Just Drive.*

# A Jingo of a Heaviness

Dear, dia]Re,

I have unauthorized news!

The state is on fire and the technical manuals have fled their offices. I am writing you now because all other coffee break channels are jammed, and I am burning from a caesura atypical to seizure.

Because of the current rate at which emergency isn't getting due credit, I have determined to raise a new machine at the speed of a very old foundation, and you [Dear { }] are at the center of the *shunk shunking* redundancy that will inform its auxiliary sound. I trust you will bode as well as a glass cog in a barrel of luminous facets here. I (picture you) splitting prettily on this new/old foundation: like a long thin crack in watery logic. Pool water logic. I look to how your swiftness will swim.

I realize. My empty platitudes aren't the ones meant to influence you. I have many requests; the facets of which are measured in angstroms, and may draw exception to my range (in empirical radius). I so have to warn you that some local obstacles have become their own race. Never less, this side winding in the sidelines; we will see, we will. Allow me to flyer this warning around town, and flag the characteristics of your cracking reach in return. To begin with.

[You will find my invitation to a celebration in a much later letter.]

For now in this dark hour I must consider your potential contribution to colonial import. Post marked, of course. Unequivocally, the languages will come to gossip over this. But, you are, after all, a careful shape that grows in correct proportion to the space you inhabit. So I don't worry the residue in the jar, or of size of tables. Let residue settle and stay behind. Let it talk back and forth to itself when the table's bumped. It is more important to be sensitive to our respiratory function and the wings of our tertiary structures [there are always three of us in every room] and the menial singularity of our structural *liquid* – music.

I feel sorry for whatever rest in an air that has not befriended your gaze. You can be an elaborately cruel apparatus! For some reason, when I think of you in an automobile; I imagine animal tongues will soon fall like hail; wildly wordless heirs of the war cry licking a lackadaisical sky. Not falling on you, necessarily, but in front and behind you in the road. Wherever there is too much slack lacking much needed practical levity. Soon the land is cumbrously littered with disembodied lingua. I sure hope I don't cringe posthumously from this hysterical aftermath.

Most death isn't much of a death.

The fact is. And, as I am so penetrable, substantively; I envy the fact. Here, I have slipped on my tidy appliances. Forgive me? You seem thinning, like a surface layer of pond water. Prone to evaporation, cloudiness, storm babble:

The more I write you, the more I write you.

All my eyes want to buy you groceries. Want to buy you food
and clothes and put you in a wooden bed in a room made of
wood. Want to weave rings of medicinal herb to string to trees
that, for now, don't yet grow around you. You bird watching,
is something I imagine. I want to untangle your view from the
technical ladders buildings conspire to clime. Speaking of this;
how easily we are interrupted. You and I.

But our hands are not as tied as our ambition is you know; so
much is possible is already a cliché under which we pretend
to agree. Instead of a volley with our dream crushed voices
wishing to spew *reductio ad absurdum*; all this could happen.

Up north, vast fields are already in private communication. The sun is an ochre tongue and lists information back and forth between each. While it is a primitive network, it will not break until the end. And in the places where the water is clean clear through; a terrific impressionism supposes its way to the bottom of a water's body. What else could it do? We crowd together in the glass bottomed vessel to observe. Our boat heels to make one wake after the next. The water talks to the water.

Be kind then. I swear I never set out meaning to demonize your beneficial obviation; I don't know how it always comes to this. Maybe it's the distant syntheses of your terms. Like a star form; you are so deliberate, fundamental, and yet nothing and barren *et* all. Time doesn't understand.

Poor time.

After you read this, and when you get to face your personal minute again; Please, please speak with your carrier pigeons. They keep dying head first in my windows! No matter how many dirty marks I leave lovingly on the glass to lessen their speed toward them. My smudged warnings are fatally unheeded.

Monday through Thursday are weapon building days, and I have no time to gather bird feathers or carcasses, or their failed deliverances from the weeded grounds outside the syllable of my

building.

And no, I can't afford groundskeepers, as many of us can't afford the convenience of hours. The weather is always much too rumor of hot ahead, and what time is it where carrier pigeon's are concerned? We are not interested in the disappointing techniques of civilization on these narrow planes; so tell your pigeons anonymity is useless.

I do plan to name a fairytale city after you after they "Never Mind." But, this week I must build a weapon of hypotheses as a model.

First things first: my two edged little weapon thinks so much of you; it cuts a forehead for you. It, it, it. That will be its exact goal.

By the way?

No longer a friend of whalebone or whalebone a friend to me, and at the accelerating pace of all systems; I may never have time to use it.

[I've wrapped a few trinkets and sent them along in a humble box, I sure hope they arrive in one piece as each still whole . . . they're for your children's pigeons.] Love,

# The daily mirrorship

It's almost November and everyone is anxious about races: different colored girls and boys go belly up for the whole band. Sleep is a rule-breaker of the game, and so the one with wind wins you points. I have been missing my sling-shot when I go out at night. But, here on the wings of a thousand optic nerves, we still owl the wee hour for whatever prey will count.

At midnight I wrote a long entry on horseback. But this morning I am afraid to look at it. I am sore from the endless galloping images. A continuous rising and falling sped up to a clutter of skittish images. Images more significant to numbers than their movements. Who returns with numbers of such radical sequences? How soon after an ecstasy so terribly aimed?

I already adore their universe and begin to compose a lyric for their kingdom in sighs.

In it, the stars seem to gesticulate the entire time, and yet they are completely likable. I don't remember how much their distinguishment weighs, but their finer points keep pace with my simple speed. However modified to manage the trite terrain. Oh the folly below! Those stars, general and normal, and yet somehow . . . a little clerical. They have been here before, and now they are all but gone. How I love all but gone.

All that is left is a shine.

I find on earth I pretend much too hard in situ: saddled as I am to thronging air. Something dramatic, something breathless about us in the wide open of it. Breathless about . . .

the files don't say what. And to be perfectly clear? I don't know how the word twinkle, when repeated twice, will relate to my interpretation of things so little.

*These are the artifacts*, I might have said, and *here I may function without certainty*. And I may have found you prey enough, and left alone slept sound again.

Yet among a lightning flash of hooves punching names to the mud; what is found but quickly gone?

Current barriers [electric/phonetic] bother me to ask; what may suddenly become of this too glorified ardency? Will it beckon a worthy mysticism, or slump to the mud like a weapon of jaw?

Today I cull the sky's cloth for picture-telling and hope the piling of these tethered selections will catalyze a furtive reaction. An oversized fire shirt or a too small heating hat. These ridiculous things I make up to wear instead of.

For your part, I thank you to mind my needle and thread. Through which you will without your camel pass, but perhaps not other than by smoke. In your place there would be wonder full enough. But, even a *duplicate* of enough would suffice. Enough of these imagined things is enough.

Against the imperceptible all I can see are bare branches: a rough sketch of how now [holy, holier] holds between such lines.

But this morning your ghost reveals an advantage. Evidenced in letters writ to me by old accomplices, wrung from banish-ment—I found—(I have found), late Tudor to Jacobean in tone: the sprawling rooms. You can't imagine my technical surprise.

There has been a tender keenness to each night's favoring of each.

This terrestrial point of view must degenerate, or else speak indelicately. Become less, well, meditative. So that arcades of lost wings disappear in a mosaic of isometric decoration. Until a trembling (enough) begins, just there, a tiny bit mean.

I surmise: Death is about. Everyone is smiles.

And life,

and *so*

## A(re) percussion of one

This is how I found my love for birds killed by housecats is
crucial to my decorating sense. *What a character* is also an aspect
of this

                                        character. [intruded up-
on].

A somewhat flirty clue: I wondered if I should separate that out
for a later entry; but alas, how summer of love. I decide.

And you, you will always agree politely because you might
not.      You will always because. Your way to answer me is
perpendicularly given to your interest in my code of questions.

I don't need to look into the wounds of fallen fruit to know I
have atomic proof. No further than this, which is also over-ripe,
or maybe a little because.

But [   ] may reply to your lampooning guesswork by playing
you back; Handwrite our comical alphabet in different cursives
on used paper bags. Say: *I like the brown ones; they go with your
nose*. And straight away, our practice alphabets will be telepathed
in a chest below the floor, to illustrate the foundation of our
mutual fantasy. The floor nearest you, of course.

I do this in spite of the spurious bulk of your unrepentant dye.

The way what you loaned me to write with is managed. It's heavier than a stage, a hammer, or a corpse. Your dye is heavier than its page.

Nothing goes in the bags. Nothing fits after the ink dries.

Down they go.

This kind of reverse erecting threatens to become sacred, but [I will] try not to balk.

I am [SHALL BE] particularizing many spiritual investments with random appointments of your trust.
Mostly, but then dream isn't as dire as the loss of it is DROLL.

So to keep my carriage light, lose my whip. Inwardly stash keys I stipulate as any locks hold, to help keep unwanted players in SUPREME suspense.

Possibly someone will return for what is left. [FOR] Less is more and more, so why collect it?

Next, in case of errant suspicions, [ ] will bet you at charades [UNDRESS]. Pantomime for you: *rust, optic, rotation, bridge*, and sinking ship. Sinking ship because I am under close observation by the clock. Those hands are filled with more air than we are FULL OF HANDS. Than verses about them are ringing; ring round some rosy

POESY.

I assure you this paragraph is a front. And as of this paragraph our slanty measurements will officially unmend our means.

[Hang hat; hang].　Some kinds of beginning are that way; And

As with any test of friendship in this game; you must
guess all
　　　my facts [act] seemly correct, and may they very well
be. Some tension is palpable, but you look simply noble in your
borrow-ed slack.

[Express delivery service. On the spot.]

Eyes at the shoulder

like to watch us take up our arrears. I know to
what I owe this view.

Despite my sudden

distancing, I think the separation between us is dependable. If
not now, with luck forthcoming.
　　　Though this whole matter is much less frugal than my

forgery of it amounts; in hindsight, I spend

the time of our life, and I assure you my aim to winsome.

not to explain: but

You are a brilliant paramour for me ever; so unlucky in
my trade. I am happier post-nightmare of each move to serve
you. Look forward, then.

Tonight I'll ring the house with blind
corners, around which I'll hide all the possibilities I can.

Until the current scheme advances: *yours*.

# The Earth Reports

[Dear: dear *dear*]

Before I collect too heavily, I walk the bended edge of some
sad song's permanence, to study a mellifluous gilding. Often
surprised how with something human I have been provided. So I
stand on my acquaintance with you. I stand on the shoulders of
my acquaintance to peek at the front of things. I ask us to climb
the short stair length to reach the height of a far romantic porch.
A height used for awe, striking a balance.

Immediately, we are faced by innocence of wind. And then the
air is filled with numberless O's for votes to cast. A cynical voice
persons up to my ears; "complete the link with permanent ink."
This may not be as funny as it is odd. I tap the shoulder. My
acquaintance, who by the way can not hear any of it, digs some
heels in.

It is autumn, and before this we traveled to the north. And in the
north we found the northern trails slept like an editor's wishing
marks. Tiny curls without hands or feet lolling in shadow. I think
we, my acquaintance and I, were impressed by the rude extent of
these witless corrections. I think we thought.

How uncareful some carefuller things wander in the wild.
Unintentionally of(f) course. Eventually, appearing paths whisper
or call aloud with green tongues for an accounting of our view.
So I must climb down from borrowed shoulders to see. I did
climb down and I descended some few stairs, until I was in,
toe to wave to creek. The creek only knew one sentence, feeling
friendly, I read along:

Everything I touch, I touch.

For sacred offerings I threw pencil shavings to the creek, and the rest of my coffee. This simple act did not appear to muddle the sentence. So sanctified, in a somewhat somber way, I returned to a table of my things. In that sun, a whitely wanting, beside empty cups. *The Telling* faced down in that sun, lie by the beer, from Portland, turning its glass mouth to Montana. I am comforted by the little glass mouth's surprise. Things like me and not alike turn warm in that sun. All except what have you caught in cool castings.

The meet that only meets a minute. In that sun I drew from hurts that occurred, between the movements of the branches. I call them hurts. How unsettling, to be covered in their droves . . . (How we truncated each other is how.)

In my highest of bones non-memory is rendered in strokes of temperature, each rubbed to life in syntheses of electric particulates, and silent. Neither made of melancholy nor tragedy, but somehow close to something satirical, or as underhanded as a light laugh.

I am described by a voice I meet there. I don't remember it.

This voice is heard from behind a wall. I know its seems; but there is no wall. Not really. And in some while I know how famously related blue is to these betweens. Some knowing soothes the littled mind. I've listened.

And now the trees are always full of shades again. Little and never landing. Love like flits of in twists the wrist. Tiny cool perils as unremarkable as the inner pleading. I listen closely to what is less. And soon there is less.

There is also a small door in the air, almost invisible, *oh much less*; pine breathing. I do not have the power or desire to shut such a door. I awake in its opening. In the last moments, the sun leaves me alone, to say it is so.

Against night I had a dream to forget my name. Though I have no filtering for such work; I had told the audience some truths. But still, the hurts, and still. I guess I was professional about my urge to show how scars behave. I think I was. I know a good deal about how scars behave. How free radicals, each dismembered as a failed fist, fly like promises looking for the confidence they need. How they consider what isn't meant, but is. Good character resides in their convoluted desire to heal. To wield is what such radicals offer; energy denied mass. Mass denied. This is as much good as wind is like to do.

I suppose.

But in the shrewd spaces between their [radicals] numbers my name does not spell correctly. So I pack my things, not knowing what else to take away. It is the spirit of a policy, not policy itself, which keeps. So I can't stay. I say I have forgotten, and am off. I make no apology, as a courtesy. To take what away and lift what to grief for thanking; is all I can. Nothing more, nothing. Yes . . . If everyone was kind I wouldn't be so afraid.

What does that mean, and what happened to her voice among them?

        [She was there, I saw her, she shining of hair and verb of blue, and all well in a vibration of rain.]

## The Difference Tone

Let's be honest. This borrowed birthright is physiologically
advantageous and drives us home to hunger. Late at night.
Slowly, and on back roads. How sick are we of pretending
where we live?

Moon    T*reeTreeTreeTreeTree.*    Moon.

You never said what I thought you would, but I listened.
I watched a world go by—so familiar it was almost ugly.
Comfort how kind radio light is; to have a place to anchor a
head's hot hum.

She said, I want music! She is the diary as arpine. She lives just
under an acre, dressed in a thin Armenian bole. She sings "tut,
tut!" and frets the air with her fingers; obvious as large white
house-flies.

I understand, but I am so American, and must play blizzard
until ashamed. Lean into my mistakes, and hear the hum. The
only étude I know takes the porch out of the banjo and gives
no quiz.

If you know what I mean you know.

Since the encryption of our mutual purpose, the difference
between the impartial and the outraged is a comparatively
small crime of passion. So small and precious, a relative kitten
of pathos. It's hardly noticeable, due to the encryption, and
though the exaggerated planting of this hedge of wreckage was
never the plan; I have grown accustomed to seeing strangers
grow banjo eyed at our site.

It's been a while now, figuring how to crawl. Along the way, accused by the smallest of silences, the somewhat perverted and invisible things suffered. And now you want to imprison me with ideas, but I'm innocently convinced: I am likening to a sigh to care. Is this a form of modern courage? The wonderfully fearful nature of hope allows what's wrong to charge my reach. I give *you* the credit for it. For your talent to steer the automobile, and for your blind bravery on these unseen roads. Funny, none of them were named except, maybe, the motherland ones.

Familiar? How far did you say home was?

Let me try and parcel this soberly. Let me attempt to trace the agony of the unanimous. Let me be discharged completely within this narrow range of flutter. Looking for the acoustic blooms—emphasized by my blood's reduction—let me go.

I am not as tired as you are, so; please, when we get home? You take the bed. It will add to its holy fluency if you become its dream form, not mine. You will add to its function as a pigeon, carrying acts-of-love messages, in part and indirectly, it may also be a right delivery system for floating limbs. Bless you: over heard thus fussing "tut, tut"—in these good terms.

Disappearance causes fellowship to combine with terrible things. Beastly angels, and rogue instigators of helpful jokes. These creatures will bind together to liberate whatever group of anyone being discharged. O science please die, *o please please science*. I must absolutely be arrested by the man playing the small guitar! I must eat my supper while the dogs wrestle under the table! I must go to the store for more butter wearing these shoes! I must scrounge for change from my dresser drawer . . .

Science, I am sorry. Let me be careful, because there is a war, because.

I am often stricken unexpectedly with soldier's heart. Not for the drama, and not because I want to resist my own abstraction. But I could swear I have imagined a digital scimitar swathing the living room screen like a blurry escape button on a giant's skull. I've heard the terrible repeating storyteller repeat instructions for encrypting the sun's job [ which is not ours: too hard, too hot], and tried to block out the lessons on how to go blind on a dime! There is a hint of violence in the repetition, and in the story's heart. I don't refer to killing just now, just the killing of it. What is made after?

Often things appear in the line of fixation and I am grazed like an open field. Stillness is less linear than light, in this light.

Then the card sorting, then the babble—

[Isn't it sad? What's become of the word Martian? It's just a piece of talk junk now . . . terribly. (If Martians never were and still might be, then why don't we keep saying so?) ]

— then, fissures grow in patterns of alms on the national pillow, until they cover whatever hermit of yellow silk, until the gallery of gibberish mimics prayers. Until, you know something, it doesn't really matter.

Funny how humility, dressed like a good political decision, goes public to dole out Technicolor souvenirs of flashy frivolity. Do you want examples? You must not get enough of it. Standing in the long lines to get into late nigh television. Early to rise; they also said.

They claim not about to make canons without the King's license and I am not to write an Ecclesiastic word without one hair of a savage bearing my lunatic remark—not before the dimming clods that stretch 688,000 miles name their hells outloud. There is no choice for us; we are a footnote on the billboard of expensive happiness.

This is such a long ride home. How far off course do you think we are?

Let's not talk a while.

What do you want to listen to now?

## Catch as can, *dear...*

The clock keeps and it is time to go places; cars go by and go places; in the cars the people are thinking of when they will need the heater, soon; and these people do not care about this diary. The song on the car radio does not care about this diary. The song on the radio is more accessible than this diary. The saguaro does not need this diary, but it scrapes its way into this diary. As for the sun rising from the hills behind. The cowboy electrician, who is on his way to fix the heaters, does not care to read this diary and without him there is no diary.

. . . This diary is older than this diary is.

## Correct thinking correcting

"It would be a 'vicious circle' for instance, to prove the 'freedom of the will' from the fact of 'personal responsibility, and then later on prove the fact of 'personal responsibility' from the principle of the 'freedom of the will'"
—from *The Science of Correct Thinking*, 1950, Celestine N. Bittle.

Why are you still listening? Haven't you learned?

You fascinate me. And how hard am I trying to please you as greatly and irresistibly; to fascinate you? It's the ultimate magic. To fascinate you to the plumb. To fascinate you to what's ahead, and not for much. To fascinate you to a bevy of secret shutters. To implicate you, and grapple with you. I grapple with you. I have to grapple.

And just as soon as I said it, I got off the phone with you and people were there and we talked, and the people left, and other people came and we talked also and then I forgot. So here then. Here is a thing I've been working on.

Please send something too.     Anything.

You.

Dear Rabbit,

Why are there so few paintings of you in the national gallery?
Unless I am mistaken, you were called, *Autumn Rhythm, Green
on Blue, The Betrothal,* and *Le Viol.* Everything but rabbit.

I was particularly offended, when perplexedly strolling along,
I came to the one they called, The Head of a Woman, after
you. But I guess we are too young to remember the days when
paintings of rabbits that did not necessarily look like rabbits
were simply called rabbits. Perhaps too many came too soon.

Painters paint rabbits like rabbits.

Still, I enjoyed looking. I hopped a staccato mile through the
galleries, to stop-and-go study you. Are you offended? Everyone
wants to know. Stop and go, stop and go. The galleries are
convenient at least.

Will you run for president this year? God, I hope. I miss
hearing your rabbit voice, your rabbit on rabbit off. The un-
rabbit sound they correct you with is deafening. Did you see
who leaps among the hills now? The natives aren't restless
because they are none. Something grassy must be done.

After the news I can't walk away. I stand behind the trees. I
just stand there. I can see the galleries through the hills and
who leaps there. After this I like things like hills and grass and
leaping. I consider everything as carefully as you are.

The galleries are so full of you, but leave useless clues. Rabbit
ears fastened to their rooftops act like some preternatural
worship. They don't pick up my complaints.

I have so many complaints.

Luckily, the computers in our area are friendly. Through them I have heard exciting rumors. I have thrown the dry recitative mentions of our failed efforts under the screen, and watch them divide to their smallest parts. Here, you ask. Here. Mentions of a future fall fall where they should.

Into the rabbit holes of digital anthems. Of course, with you in mind;

I am watching my step.

In my view neither consumers' goods nor contraband are swift enough to move without force. The destruction of evidence of God is proof; or how do we expect corn gets to where corn doesn't grow? And how long did the traveling salesman know?

Sway, sway (all day every day):

Right rabbit?

Which virtue was it that supplied the congregation with enough fear to cast out the possibility of God's love for homosexuals and work-a-day perverts? Most of that original tenderness has hardened. Is economy of such things so necessary? Economy has nothing to do with ecosystems anyway, systems of down to earthiness. Systems of fever, safety, sovereignty. There are lessons to cure this; but they are an endless quiz. Like the one the congregation (also referred to as *the survivors*) have creeping up on them. It is sad to watch them gape that way. Frozenly gaping into that terrible hole in their rhapsodic glut. What's *down* there anyway?

Do you know rabbit?

In your line of work, as master craftsman of triangular psalms and fleets of supplication, what do you consider is your dearest virtue? Velum, veil or sail?

Are you really wedded to your poverty so much rabbit?

I do not mean to exploit the nomad rabbit, but during my sagacious rummagings I found warm dovetails hugging the mud of deep doors, and recognized in them the polilineal— and innocently faceted—shapes of our prairie tribe. I found they resembled visages of a vagrant geometric heaven, almost appearing in conference—or confluence with our most tender will. An amity of cruel purity and heroic violence, between which fleeting nuances shuddered like the restless hearts of worker bees.

You agree that broken matters reign on this plain don't you?

Which one do you want to be first Rabbit? Jesus or God?
Remember, most rabbits would rather reach for a remnant than
pray toward the rising fog each morn. But believe me, I'm all
set. I mean, we are all all set. Either way, I heard someone say
that God is dead you know? I heard someone wrote it. Heard it
was published. Think I've got a copy or two stored in my hutch.

I miss you rabbit. But I know you and I are impossible without
love.

When bird came by today I made it a point to ask how good it
was to live in a nest this size, and bird just answered, "Chirp."
Honestly rabbit; you know how bird is always mocking.

Nothing more was said between us. She cocked her head,
and then flapped her wings a few times and was gone out the
nearest open window. Back into the wild blue.

I wasn't kidding when I said I didn't know what the world was
coming to. But I keep hopping. I put all my memories of you;
the way you smell, the way you taste, the way you cry – in my
hindgut for best keeping. Please don't feel guilty having to hang
your music upside down in your hole, rabbit. Your big big hole
of a house.

## The Author

Aidan Fine grew up in the house that his paternal great grandfather built in the small mountain town of Prescott, Arizona. His poems have appeared in the journals *Diner, Nocturnes Review of Literary Arts, Sonora Review, Cue,* online at *No Tell Motel, La Fovea* and *The Drunken Boat,* and elsewhere. He attended undergraduate school at The University of Tampa in Florida, and graduated with an MFA from Bennington Writing Seminars in Vermont, where he studied poetry and architectural history and theory. He has been the director of two community writing centers, Casa Libre en la Solana in Tucson, Arizona which he also co-founded, and InkTank World Headquarters in Cincinnati, Ohio. Along with artifice rhetoric and postmodern theory, Aidan's passions include architecture and the history of fools/folly/and other humorous literary fodder.

*Author photo by Kate Street.*